I0799061

Ted's List

by Antonio Colantoni
illustrated by Mary Maass

Core Decodable 39

Bothell, WA • Chicago, IL • Columbus, OH • New York, NY

MHEonline.com

Send all inquiries to:
McGraw-Hill Education
8787 Orion Place
Columbus, OH 43240

ISBN: 978-0-02-143332-2
MHID: 0-02-143332-1

Printed in the United States of America.

9 10 11 12 KOD 24

Ted printed his list.

Ted read his list.

Then, Ted got bread and milk.

Then, Dad read.

Dad got jam instead of apricots.

Dad and Ted then headed back.

Dad fixed eggs.
Then, Ted spread jam on bread.

"I dreamt of jam and bread!"